W9-AZX-750

Internet Power Research Using the Big6™ Approach

Revised Edition

THE INTERNET LIBRARY

Internet Power Research Using the Big6™ Approach

Revised Edition

Art Wolinsky

Enslow Publishers, Inc.

40 Industrial Road	PO Box 38
Box 398	Aldershot
Berkeley Heights, NJ 07922	Hants GU12 6BP
USA	UK

http://www.enslow.com

*To my wonderful wife Jill, who has
always given me the support and freedom
to pursue my dreams and ideas.*

Copyright © 2005 by Art Wolinsky
Original edition © 2002 by Art Wolinsky

Big6 trademark pending; Big6 model, copyright © 1987, Michael Eisenberg
and Robert Berkowitz, used with permission.

All rights reserved.

No part of this book may be reproduced by any means without the written
permission of the publisher.

Library of Congress Cataloging-in-Publication Data

Wolinsky, Art.
    Internet power research using the Big6 approach / Art Wolinsky.—
Rev. ed.
        p. cm. — (The Internet library)
    Includes bibliographical references and index.
    ISBN 0-7660-1564-5 (pbk)
    ISBN 0-7660-1563-7 (library ed.)
    1. Computer network resources—Juvenile literature. 2. Research—
Methodology—Juvenile literature. 3. Electronic information resource
literacy—Juvenile literature. I. Title. II. Series.
ZA4380.W65 2005
025.04—dc22
                                   2004022185

Printed in the United States of America

10 9 8 7 6 5 4 3 2 1

To Our Readers:
We have done our best to make sure all Internet Addresses in this book were
active and appropriate when we went to press. However, the author and the
publisher have no control over and assume no liability for the material
available on those Internet sites or on other Web sites they may link to. Any
comments or suggestions can be sent by e-mail to comments@enslow.com
or to the address on the back cover.

Trademarks:
Most computer and software brand names have trademarks or registered
trademarks. The individual trademarks have not been listed here.

Cover Photo: Index Stock Imagery, Inc./Benelux Press.

Contents

The Big6™ Skills Overview

Step 1. Task Definition
1.1 Define the information problem
1.2 Identify information needed in order to complete the task (to solve the information problem)

Step 2. Information Seeking Strategies
2.1 Determine the range of possible sources (brainstorm)
2.2 Evaluate the different possible sources to determine priorities (select the best sources)

Step 3. Location and Access
3.1 Locate sources (intellectually and physically)
3.2 Find information within sources

Step 4. Use of Information
4.1 Engage (e.g., read, hear, view, touch) the information in a source
4.2 Extract relevant information from a source

Step 5. Synthesis
5.1 Organize information from multiple sources
5.2 Present the information

Step 6. Evaluation
6.1 Judge the product (effectiveness)
6.2 Judge the information problem-solving process (efficiency)

Introduction: The Big6™ Approach and Internet Power Research

T his is my friend Web. He will be appearing throughout the pages of this book to guide you through the information presented here and to take you to a variety of Internet sites and activities. Web is an important part of our rapidly changing world. Though many things are changing, nothing is changing more rapidly than computers and the Internet.

▶ Information Overload

When I was a student, I can remember the biggest problem I had when a teacher assigned a report was finding information. If I didn't get to the library right away, the books and magazines were already signed out. Today with the Internet, too little information is not the problem. The problem is information overload. When you do a search, you can get hundreds, thousands, or even millions of hits on your topic. Handling that can be a problem.

Another problem I faced in school was something I call process overload. I would go into English class and the teacher would try to help us by giving us a method to do our research and our reports. Then I would go into Social Studies and the teacher would try to help us by giving us a method to do our reports. Then I would go into Science and the teacher would again try to help us by giving us a method to do our reports. The problem was that each method was slightly different and all that help was confusing me instead of helping me.

Two friends of mine, Mike Eisenberg and Bob Berkowitz, had the same kind of problems. They decided to develop a single method that students, teachers, parents, and just about anyone could use to solve ANY kind of information problem. It didn't matter whether it was a report, organizing your schedule, doing your chores, or picking a birthday

Big6 Creators

The Big6 Research Method was created by Mike Eisenberg (right) and Bob Berkowitz (left).

present for your Aunt Tilly. If the problem involved information, you could solve it using their method.

Web and I are going to show you how the Big6 method of problem solving can make your life easier. It will help you handle information overload and process overload.

▶ The Big6 Research Method

So, fire up your Web browser and head to the Big6 Web site to see the basics of the Big6. This is what we saw when we visited the kids' page on the Big6 site, <http://www.big6.com/kids>.

This book will show you how to use the Big6 Research Method and the Internet to do power

On Your Screen

This is the opening page of the Big6 Web site for kids.

research to solve your problems. You do not need a computer or Internet connection to read this book. But to then put the Big6 to use and do your own research on the Internet, you will need both a computer and the Internet. First, Web and I want to tell you a little more about computers, the Internet, and the Big6. It is good background, so keep reading.

▶ A Brief History of Computers

Software companies are putting out new versions faster than ever before. It seems like every time I turn around I am helping Web upgrade a piece of software or put on the latest operating system.

About thirty years ago, the early computers had 6,000 transistors and could handle about 640,000 instructions in one second. Does that seem like a lot of transistors and speed? Well, back in 1974 it was, but in just about thirty short years, things certainly have changed.

Today, computers have more than 40 million transistors and can handle more than a BILLION instructions per second. Now that is impressive! What is more impressive is that there is no end in sight. In years to come, the numbers will keep rising.

Computers today are a million times more powerful than the computers of twenty years ago and twenty years from now, the computers will be a million times more powerful than the ones today.

Web visited the How Stuff Works Web site, grabbed some information, and

The Big6 also has software called Big6 TurboTools. This software takes you through each step and provides helpful hints along the way. Ask your teacher or librarian if your school or library has TurboTools.

Big6 TurboTools™

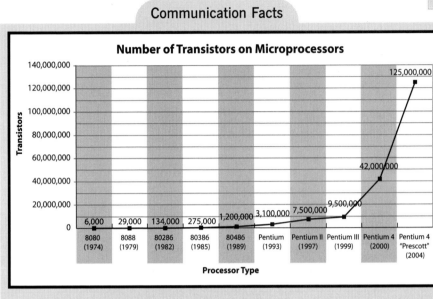

Communication Facts

Number of Transistors on Microprocessors

The growth of the number of transistors follows the evolution of microprocessor chips and computer power.

displayed a graph on his screen that showed the explosive growth of transistors on microprocessors over the years.

▶ The Information Explosion

Computers allow us to process information at speeds that were unimaginable a few years ago. As a result, the amount of information is growing at such a fantastic rate, it is almost impossible to imagine.

To give you an idea, let me ask you a question. If you went to school with Christopher Columbus, how much information would you come in contact with compared with what you do today?

According to Richard S. Wurman, author of *Information Anxiety*, the daily *New York Times* contains more information than Columbus would have come across in his entire lifetime! Does that give you an idea of how information is growing?

There are so many changes taking place and so much information to cover in this book that it can not all fit on these pages. So we are going to use the Internet to help us. After you read the book, you can visit <http://www.big6.com/> for more information and for updates on information contained here.

If that does not impress you, perhaps this will. If I offered you a thousand dollars to read all the scientific information printed yesterday, would you take the job?

Before you answer that question and start planning on how to spend your money, you might like to know that Professor B.L. Spiegel tells us that each day enough scientific information is printed to fill seven full sets of the *Encyclopedia Britannica*.

I guess you'll turn down that job, but you should be getting an idea of how rapidly information is growing. Just in case you need more convincing, consider this: According to a University of California at Berkeley study, in 2002 about five exabytes of information was stored on print, film, magnetic, and optical media. Of course that might not mean much until I tell you that five exabytes is equal to all the words ever spoken by all the humans in the world since the beginning of time!

Are you beginning to get the idea?

▶ The Pattern Continues

After last Thanksgiving dinner, Web and I were visiting with my grown-up children and some of

Communication Facts

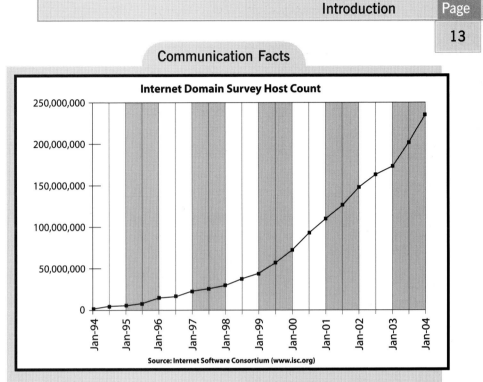

Internet Domain Survey Host Count

Source: Internet Software Consortium (www.isc.org)

The growth of the Internet is shown through this graph of host Web sites.

my nieces and nephews who are in middle school. We were talking about school, how some things have stayed the same, and how some have changed dramatically.

One thing that has stayed the same is doing research and reports, but the way today's students go about doing the work has changed in many ways. The biggest changes are due to computers and the Internet. When I went to school, we did not have computers and we did not have the Internet. I had to depend on the school library and as you know, my biggest problem was often finding enough information.

My son and daughter had it easier in the early 1990s. They did not have the Internet either, but

There are all kinds of graphs, charts, and statistics about how much information is out there. Here are a few places you can go for more information about more information!

The Atlas of Cyber Geography and graphic representations of the Internet.
<http://www.cybergeography.org/atlas/atlas.html>

Here's the latest University of California at Berkeley research on how much information is out there.
<http://www.sims.berkeley.edu/research/projects/how-much-info-2003/>

This site gives a breakdown of Internet population by country and language.
<http://www.glreach.com/globstats/index.php3>

the libraries had many more books. They also had CD-ROM collections, and used word processors and printers. Their biggest problem was getting to a computer and CD that was available.

Today you, and my nieces and nephews, have the Internet and a completely different set of tools, which creates a completely different set of problems. My nieces and nephews said that their problem is too much information. A lot of it is too hard to understand, a lot of it is inaccurate, and a lot of it is just plain junk. They sometimes have a hard time figuring out what to use and what not to use.

My niece, Alisha, said that it seems like every time she does a search on the Internet she comes up with more information than she could read in her entire lifetime. Her class was doing a project on endangered species and she had picked blue whales. When she did an Internet search for blue whales at Google, <http://www.google.com>, she came up with 274,000 articles (hits) in less than one second! She figured out that even if she could visit one site a minute, it would take her one hundred

How Do I Do That?

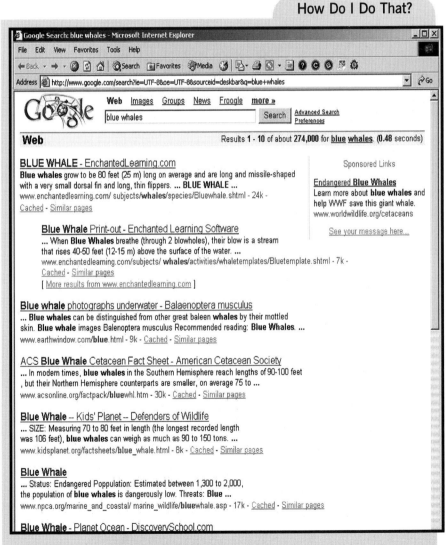

When Alisha did a search for "blue whales" on Google, she came up with 274,000 hits.

ninety days to go through all of them, even if she worked twenty-four hours a day and never slept!

At this point, my nephew, Jared chimed in. "You think you have problems? My teachers must think I am a computer, because they give me so much to do. Besides my every day homework, music lessons, soccer practice, and chores, I have reports due in two different classes. Then they think they are helping us by giving us a method to do the reports, but the methods are different and it only makes even more work! It would be nice if I had more time for video games, to watch TV, or to play with my friends.

"How can I get everything done? Unless I can narrow down the information and figure out how to put everything together, I will never be done in time. I am not a robot. There is just too much to do!"

Web and I looked at each other and smiled. We knew that we could help them solve their problems.

▶ Understanding the Big6™ Steps

Web and I took Alisha and Jared to the kids page of the Big6 Web site that we told you about earlier and showed them the steps. I explained to them how each step fit into the process and how all the steps together could help them solve their problems.

Step 1 is **Task Definition**. This is when you define your job, including questions that need to be answered, the kinds of information needed, and how much you need. This may mean picking a topic for a school report and narrowing it down, or figuring out how to plan a birthday party. Sometimes you need a lot of information from many different sources and other times you may need just one or two pieces of information.

Step 2 is **Information Seeking Strategies**. This means thinking of all the different ways that you could find the information you need and then picking the best ones.

Step 3 is **Location and Access**. This means actually finding the sources of the information. This is when you figure out all the places that might have what you need and figure out how to get the information.

Step 4 is **Use of Information**. Now it's time to dig in and learn the material. You may end up reading it, listening to it, looking at it, touching it, tasting it, or doing other things that will help you understand it better. Taking notes is very important so that you can organize the information later.

Step 5 is **Synthesis**. This is the toughest part. You have to put everything together in a way that makes sense to you and to other people. It's time to put all of your facts together to solve your problem. This may mean creating a report, throwing a party, or any other problem you need to solve.

Step 6 is **Evaluation**. It is the last step in the process, but you can use it in combination with the other Big6 steps. Even after you have solved the problem, it is important for you to go back and figure out how well you did and to look for ways to improve the next time you have a problem to solve.

Big6™ Steps   Communication Facts   On Your Screen

The Big6™ Skills Overview

Step 1. Task Definition

1.1 Define the information problem

1.2 Identify information needed in order to complete the task (to solve the information problem)

Step 2. Information Seeking Strategies

2.1 Determine the range of possible sources (brainstorm)

2.2 Evaluate the different possible sources to determine priorities (select the best sources)

Step 3. Location and Access

3.1 Locate sources (intellectually and physically)

3.2 Find information within sources

Step 4. Use of Information

4.1 Engage (e.g., read, hear, view, touch) the information in a source

4.2 Extract relevant information from a source

Step 5. Synthesis

5.1 Organize information from multiple sources

5.2 Present the information

Step 6. Evaluation

6.1 Judge the product (effectiveness)

6.2 Judge the information problem-solving process (efficiency)

▶ It Begins to Makes Sense

Jared and Alisha thought that it made sense, because they were already doing similar steps in the methods their teachers gave them. Still, they were not sure why they needed to follow the Big6 whenever they had a problem to solve.

We then talked about how the brain works. It does not matter what the job, problem, or task is, the more you do something the better you get at it. It does not matter whether it is hitting a baseball, playing a computer game, or doing math. The more you do things the better you get.

Doing things over and over the same way actually causes changes in the chemicals and connections in the brain. Eventually, the pathways are so well marked that you do things automatically without thinking about it.

Think about multiplication tables or video games. With practice the times tables become automatic. With computer games, your fingers seem to work by themselves. You use the pathways in your brain that deal with math or the game so often that they allow impulses to travel faster and faster. The same is true for many other school tasks, but that is only part of the reason for using the Big6.

▶ A Common Vocabulary

You get better at computer games by talking about them with your friends. You get better at schoolwork by talking about it with your classmates. Working with others helps you get better at anything, and part of the reason is because you are all using the same vocabulary. You are using terms and definitions that you are all familiar with.

If adults were listening to your conversation about computer games, it would sound like a foreign language to them. They would have to stop you after every third word to ask what you mean.

You and your friends share a common vocabulary and a common way of doing things that allows you to get right down to solving the problem and getting better at the game.

It is the same way with the Big6. It gives you a common vocabulary for solving information problems. When you work with other Big6ers and use terms like Task Definition, Information Seeking Strategies, and Synthesis, you all know what they mean and you can use that common vocabulary to get things done quickly and efficiently.

Jared smirked a little and said, "OK, let us give it a try. Can you show us how the Big6 and Internet can help us solve our problems so we can get to play those video games?"

Chapter 1

Step 1:
Task Definition

1.1 Define the information problem
1.2 Identify information needed in order to complete the task (to solve the information problem)

▶ What Is the Problem?

The first step in the Big6 Research Method is defining the problem that you need to solve. Then you have to figure out what information you will need. The Big6 can be a powerful research tool for solving any problem you might have—even things you may not have thought of as problems. It can help you to do research for a school project, plan events, buy a birthday present, or pick a new hairstyle.

Alisha's class was studying endangered species. Their teacher asked them to do some research on their own and teach the class about what they had learned. Then, they would work as a class to come up with a plan they could put into action to help save one or more endangered species.

Jared said his social studies assignment to plan a family vacation was really cool, because his family was going on vacation over the winter break. He could do a project that was really useful! Part of his problem was that half of the family wanted to go someplace that had winter sports and the other half wanted warm weather, sun, and surf.

▶ Getting to the Task

I had an idea of what Alisha and Jared were doing, but I needed more details and I asked them if their teachers had given any more instructions. They both had copies of the "official" assignments.

Alisha's assignment paper said:

Endangered Species

By now, you have an idea of the endangered species problems and have an endangered animal you wish to see protected.

You must become an "expert" on that animal by doing research. Then you must make an oral presentation to convince the class that your animal is the one we should adopt as our class project to help protect.

As part of your oral presentation, you must use some sort of multimedia presentation. You may use *PowerPoint*, *HyperStudio*, *SuperLink*, or a product created by another program, as long as it can run on our computers without having to install special software.

Jared's assignment read:

A Family Vacation

Many students think vacations are something you just go on and they do not require much planning. Your job will be to plan a one-week vacation for a family of four. You can go anywhere and do anything that you want. You have a $5,000 budget for food, travel, lodging, activities, and souvenirs.

Internet Addresses | Communication Facts | How Do I Do That?

If you want to do some research on endangered species, here are some good starting places.

EELink is an environmental site that has a great endangered species section with links to dozens of top quality resources.
<http://eelink.net/EndSpp/>

The National Environmental Directory lists more than 13,000 organizations that you can call, visit, or write to.
<http://environmentaldirectory.net/>

EndangeredSpecie.com has information designed for students and teachers.
<http://www.endangeredspecie.com/>

If you are going to a foreign country you must have passports and any necessary shots. These things usually take time and money, but for this assignment we will assume you have the passports and shots.

We will also assume that you already have all the equipment you would need if you are going camping or participating in sports like skiing or surfing.

Are you starting to see that a vacation must be carefully planned?

Your final product will be in two parts. The first will be a brochure that will highlight the things you think will sell your family on your vacation. The second will be a spreadsheet that shows all your costs for your trip. You will also create an itinerary, a schedule of events, which will include all the details for your trip (flight information, hotel information, activities, and so on). Your spreadsheet and itinerary should include, but not be limited to, the following items:

Transportation

If you are flying, you must include those costs as well as flight information (airline, flight numbers, and times). You must also include the cost to rent a car at your destination.

If you are driving, you must include a map with your route. The cost of gas for your trip should be figured at $.07 a mile.

Lodging

Include hotel costs for your stay at your final destination, as well as overnight stays along the way if you are driving a long distance.

Meals

Show the number of meals per day times the number of people going, times the number of days you will be gone, times the average cost of a meal for one person.

Activities

Show which activities will be done on which days and the cost for each activity.

There are many additional expenses that people tend to forget about that must be figured into your budget. Many flights and rental cars have fees or taxes that will need to be included. You are also probably going to want to bring home some souvenirs. It is also a good idea to set some money aside in case something unexpected occurs, such as a lost piece of luggage.

▶ Alisha's Task

Now that Web and I had an idea of what Alisha and Jared were doing, I said to Alisha, "What do you have to do?"

She crinkled her nose and said, "I already told you. I have to do research on blue whales. Remember the 274,000 hits?"

I smiled and said, "Yes, I remember, but is that what your teacher told you to do? Did she tell you to do blue whale research?"

"Well, no, not really. We already saw a movie on endangered species that gave us some background material. Right now, we are doing the individual research described on the paper. . . . Oh, I get it now!

On Your Screen

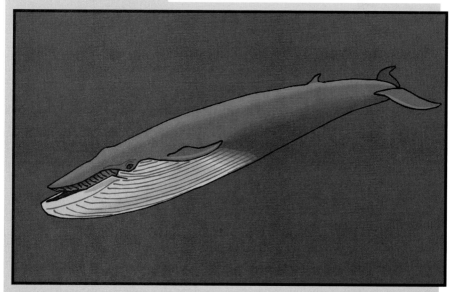

The blue whale is the largest animal that ever lived. Humans hunted the blue whale to near extinction until the mid-1960s when many countries agreed to stop hunting the whales.

I have to do research, but that is not my final task. My actual job is to make a speech and presentation that will convince the class that my animal is the one we should work to save."

Alisha had completed the first part of Task Definition. She knew that her job was to make a presentation that convinced the class that her animal is the one they should save. The second part of this step is to figure out what kind of information was needed to solve the problem.

Alisha, Jared, Web, and I discussed the kinds of information she would need. We came up with things like general information about the animal's life and habits, where it lived, what makes it endangered, why it is important to save, and things we can do to save the animal.

Finally, we discussed how much information she needed. This was important because she already knew that there was more information than she could possibly handle. We decided that if she came up with three or four sources that had a lot of good information it would be enough.

▶ Jared's Task

I turned to Jared and said, "OK, Jared. Let us figure out your task."

He said, "Before we started learning about the Big6, I would have said that my task was to plan a family vacation, but now I know that is not entirely correct. My task is to create a spreadsheet of all of the costs, along with an itinerary that includes the trip details, and make a brochure to highlight the points that will convince my family to take the vacation."

"What about the other half of Task Definition?" I asked. "What kinds of information do you need and how much do you need?"

He thought for a moment and said, "Well, it looks like the teacher really helped us with that part of Task Definition, because she told us what kind of information we need for the project."

He went on to say, "I really need a lot of information, but I don't need it from a lot of different places, because my mother makes that part easy."

That remark puzzled me and I asked him how his mother made it easy. He laughed and explained that his mother was afraid of flying and that any vacation they went on would have to be one where they drive.

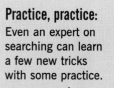

Practice, practice: Even an expert on searching can learn a few new tricks with some practice.

He said that in New Jersey where he lived, there were plenty of great seashore resorts for a sand and surf vacation, but they wouldn't get much of a tan and the water would be a bit cold in the middle of December. If they wanted water sports, they would have to drive to Florida, but he didn't want to spend half his vacation in a car. So he decided to

convince his family that a winter sports vacation was the way to go.

He said, "That makes New England or Canada the most likely place for winter sports. That means I have to research the best places to go, make sure they can be done with the $5,000 budget, get prices for all the items on the teacher's list, create the spreadsheet, write the itinerary, and make the brochure."

He smiled and added, "The Task Definition part of Big6 really makes you think about what you need. Even though it's the first part of the process, it made me think about the end product and all the steps in between that I would have to do to complete the task. That's really cool!"

▶ Where Was Web?

During the Task Definition discussion, Web was very quiet. When I asked him why, he told us that the Internet does not always play a major role in Task Definition, especially in this case.

This time the students had been told by their teachers what the task was. In some cases the Internet could help if people are not all together in the same location. They could use e-mail or instant messaging to have discussions, or use other software to talk to each other over the Internet.

"Don't worry," Web said, "I will have plenty to say in the upcoming steps."

Chapter 2

Step 2: Information Seeking Strategies

2.1 Determine the range of possible sources (brainstorm)

2.2 Evaluate the different possible sources to determine priorities (select the best sources)

Once you understand the task, you have to figure out every place you might find information about the topic. Then narrow the list down to the best possible sources. You might want to try a process called brainstorming.

Brainstorming is a way of generating many ideas in a short time. People use brainstorming in schools, businesses, and government. Everyone from kindergartners on up to the President can use it.

During brainstorming, you follow a simple set of rules:

1. You accept EVERY idea. No idea is too strange. Sometimes the strange ideas turn out to be the best and other times they spark great ideas. Of course there is a big difference between strange ideas and silliness. Brainstorming is fun, but it is serious work. Stick to the job.

2. You do not discuss any ideas until AFTER brainstorming is over. Discussing ideas slows the process and discourages some people from giving ideas. You accept every idea without commenting on them until after you finish brainstorming.

3. It is OK to take someone's idea and change it a little. This is called piggybacking.

Web's screen lit up and he said, "I told you I would be saying a lot starting with this step! There is software known as concept-mapping or mind-mapping software. It can speed the job and make it easier. Concept mapping is a way of organizing your ideas so that you can look at them more easily.

"I will show you how it works. As you brainstorm, I will use concept-mapping software to record your ideas. I will use a program called *Inspiration* to do Alisha's brainstorming. Of course, other software packages do concept mapping. You can also use a word processor or even pencil and paper."

All three of us started coming up with ideas of where to look for information on blue whales and on the next page is what Web did with our ideas.

Internet Addresses Communication Facts How Do I Do That?

The Internet can really help. Here are links to a few sites that tell about how to make concept maps and point you to other sites that have information about concept mapping. (You might want to show them to your teachers.)

<http://users.edte.utwente.nl/lanzing/cm_home.htm>

<http://www.coun.uvic.ca/learn/program/hndouts/map_ho.html>

<http://www.graphic.org/concept.html>

How Do I Do That?

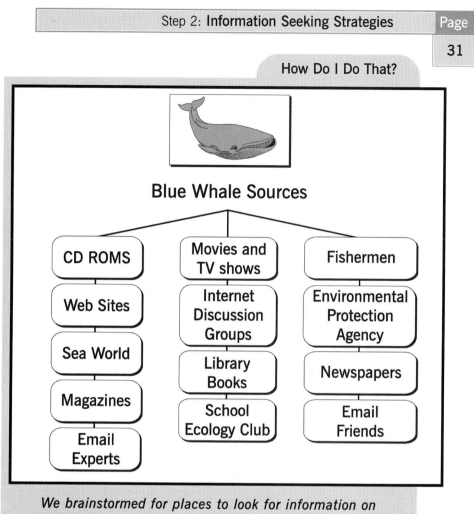

Blue Whale Sources

CD ROMS

Movies and
TV shows

Fishermen

Web Sites

Internet
Discussion
Groups

Environmental
Protection
Agency

Sea World

Library
Books

Newspapers

Magazines

School
Ecology Club

Email
Friends

Email
Experts

*We brainstormed for places to look for information on
blue whales.*

▶ Narrowing Down the Sources

The second part of this step is to begin narrowing
the sources down to the ones you want to use. You
might have a long list of ideas from your brainstorming. Pick the ones that seem like they will
be the most helpful. If you have used a concept-
mapping program, you can just move the ideas
around on the screen. Put the best ideas on one side
and the ideas you probably won't use on the other
side of the screen.

Alisha noted that during Task Definition we decided that she would not need many sources, so we decided to put the ones she might use in the order that she would follow. She wanted to use the computer as much as possible, because she thought that would be a time saver. With the computer, she could visit Web sites and check the school's online card catalog to locate books and CDs at the school library.

Web moved things around as we discussed them. This is the result.

How Do I Do That?

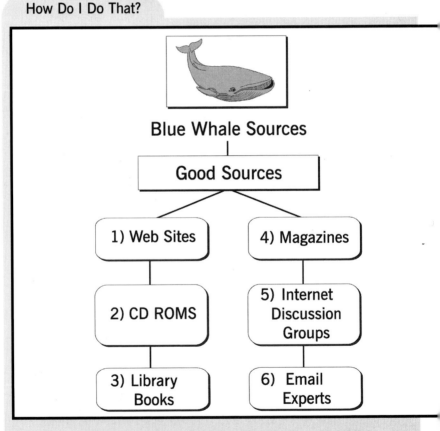

We organized the ideas and put them in the order Alisha would follow.

On Your Screen

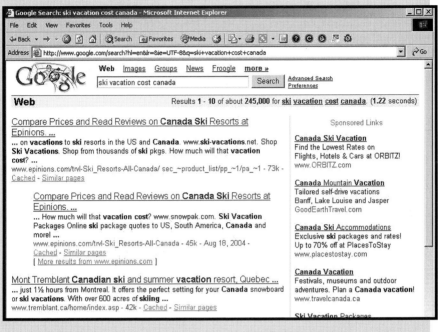

A search for "ski vacation cost canada" on Google.com looked like this.

▶ A Different Strategy

Jared's information requirements were different than Alisha's. She would probably have to locate information from more sources than Jared, and Jared had a budget that would have a lot to do with his final product.

As we spoke, it was clear there were a number of places he could look for his information. He could use the Internet, an atlas, or ask his father to contact his automobile club. Actually, he could use the Internet to locate all of his information including the atlas and the automobile club. Without even thinking about it, we had gone from Task Definition right into Information Seeking Strategies.

Chapter 3

Step 3: Location and Access

3.1 Locate sources (intellectually and physically)
3.2 Find information within sources

The next step in the Big6 is to find the material needed for the project. Sometimes this means a trip to the library, searching through card catalogs and trying to locate the material on the shelves, but today computers and the Internet make your search a lot easier. You can search through a lot of information quickly using the Internet. It's easy to see why using the Big6 and the Internet together can help you do power research!

You may be able to search your school library card catalog online. That's a good place to start. Larger county libraries may also have online catalogs. If you don't find what you need there, you can do a search on the World Wide Web.

Alisha searched her school's online library card catalog using the word "whale." She found twenty-six books. You can see at a glance that there are books that will help her.

▶ On to the World Wide Web

Once we checked the libraries, we decided to begin looking for information on the World Wide Web.

On Your Screen

Library
Search

Enter search words: whale

Keyword | Title | Author | Subject | Series | Call # | Power | Limiters | Bookbag | Help

Keyword Search: whale

Titles 1 - 25 of 26   0 Items in Bookbag

Title	Author	Call Number	Status
Gone a-whaling	Murphy, Jim, 1947-	306.3 MUR	IN
The humpback whale.	Green, Carl R.	599.51 Gre	IN
Hunters of the whale	Kirk, Ruth.	970.3 Kir	IN
In the wake of the whale.	Barbour, John Andrews, 1928-	599 Bar	IN
Inside the whale and other animals.	Parker, Steve.	591 Par	IN
The Sea World book of whales.	Bunting, Eve, 1928-	599.5 Bun	IN
A whale for the killing.	Mowat	599 Mow	IN
The whale in fact and in fiction..	Moffett, Robert Knight.	599 Mof	IN
Whales.	Berger, Gilda.	599.5 Ber	IN
Whales of the world.	Clapham, Phil.	599.5 CLA	IN

This is what Alisha came up with when she searched her school library card catalog online using the word "whale."

Jared and Alisha had learned a few search techniques from their teachers, but Web and I felt that we should give them (and you) a few more tips about using search engines on the Internet.

Searching the Internet is different than searching for books. When Alisha searched the card catalog she found that using the word "blue" narrowed the search too much. Just searching for "whale" gave her 26 books. However, when she searched the Internet for "whales" she got 1,610,000 hits. Even after she narrowed the search to "blue whales" she came up with 274,000 hits.

A good thing about using search engines is that if you use good search techniques, you can locate

Internet Addresses | Communication Facts | How Do I Do That?

Here are some sites to learn more about useful search techniques:

The KidsClick! World of Web Searching is a project of the Ramapo Catskills Library System.
< http://www.rcls.org/wows/>

The Oregon State Library System has a great tutorial for kids.
< http://www.oslis.k12.or.us/elementary/howto/findinfo/>

Library books and your school's Web page are great places to start your research.

the Web site and often zoom right in on the part of the site that has the information you need. In other words, you can do Location and Access at the same time!

There are quite a few techniques you might use to search more successfully. Unfortunately, we do not have time to go over all of them now, but I will have Web point you to places on the Internet where you can find out about them and sharpen your skills. In the meantime, I will give you an overview and a few tips.

A great place to start your search is an educational database at your library or accessed from your school Web page. It will send you to useful, reliable Web sites and information.

▶ Engines and Indexes

There are actually many different types of search tools, but for our purposes we will group them into three major categories: search engines, subject trees (also known as search indexes), and meta search tools (search many search engines at one time). If you know the differences between them, you will be able to choose the best tool for the job.

Search engines use computer programs to gather their information and create their index. This allows them to create millions and millions of entries. Unfortunately, computers do not always do a good job of indexing because they are not intelligent (except for Web).

Human beings, not computers, create *subject trees*. A person visits each site and indexes it. Of course, humans cannot do things as quickly as computers and subject trees have much fewer entries than search engines. Therefore, you will get fewer hits. However, the hits are often more useful than those returned by a search engine.

Meta search tools are search engines or computer programs that search a collection of search engines or indexes. You often use meta search tools when you are looking for hard-to-find information.

The tools you use are determined by the kind of information you are seeking. Information that is not unusual and that many people often seek can

| Internet Addresses | Communication Facts | How Do I Do That? |

Search engines: Computer programs that gather information and create their index.

Subject trees: Human beings gather information and create the index.

Meta search tools: These search other search engines and indexes.

be found easily in a search index. For harder to find information, a search engine may be better.

▶ What Is Important and What Is Not

In order to zoom in on the information you want, you must first understand how search engines create their indexes and how to think like the index.

Search engines create their indexes by looking at the words on a page and creating the index based on words that it considers important and unimportant. Common words such as "and," "of," "is," "for," "the," and many others are ignored because they will appear on almost any page.

Words that are unusual and words that appear multiple times on a page are important. These are the words used in creating the index.

Now, think like a search engine. If you visit a page that has the information you want, use some of their *key words* in your next search.

Internet Addresses   Communication Facts   How Do I Do That?

Here are some popular search tools for kids.

KidsClick	<http://www.kidsclick.org/>
Yahooligans	<http://www.yahooligans.com>
Ask Jeeves for Kids	<http://www.ajkids.com>

If you don't find what you are looking for at the kid's sites, here are my favorite tools.

Google	<http://www.google.com>
Hotbot	<http://www.hotbot.lycos.com/?query=>
Yahoo	<http://www.yahoo.com>
Ask Jeeves	<http://www.askjeeves.com>

▶ Using Search Engine Sign Language

You should know that when you type more than one word in the search it will look for those words wherever they appear on the page, but not all search tools look for the words the same way.

Alisha needed information about "blue whales." If she typed those two words, she would get information about blue whales and a lot of useless information. For example, she might get a page that talks about a hotel or restaurant with that name. Some search tools will even give pages that have only one of the words.

One answer is to give exact directions to the search engine using Boolean logic. Boolean math and logic is a way of using words and symbols to show the relationship between words and numbers. You will probably learn about basic Boolean logic and math in high school. Web will tell you where you can get more information.

You can use three simple symbols to make very powerful searches. They are quotation marks, the plus sign, and the minus sign.

"phrase"	Find those exact words or phrase.
+word	This word must be on the page.
−word	Ignore the page if this word is on it.

If you surround a phrase in quotes, it tells the search engine to look for the words exactly as they appear. If you put a + in front of a word, it tells the search engine that the word must be on the page. If you put a − in front, it tells the search engine to ignore the page if that word appears on it.

Web did some searching at Altavista (search engine), Google

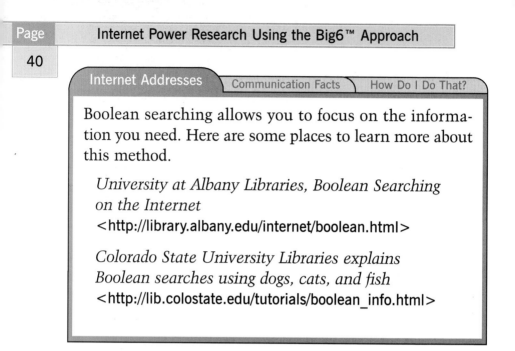

Internet Addresses | Communication Facts | How Do I Do That?

Boolean searching allows you to focus on the information you need. Here are some places to learn more about this method.

University at Albany Libraries, Boolean Searching on the Internet
<http://library.albany.edu/internet/boolean.html>

Colorado State University Libraries explains Boolean searches using dogs, cats, and fish
<http://lib.colostate.edu/tutorials/boolean_info.html>

(meta search engine), and Yahoo (search index). We can look at the results and see how different terms and different search tools make a big difference.

Search Term	Altavista	Google	Yahoo
blue whales	634,000	274,000	24
+blue +whales	634,000	274,000	24
"blue whales"	57,900	32,400	9
-blue +whales	1,890,000	916,000	625

Wow! Altavista has 634,000 hits and Yahoo has only 24. There are many reasons for the differences in this chart. One reason is that when you use two or more words without signs or quotes, it can mean different things to different search tools, which explains some of the difference between Altavista and Google. The rest of the difference between them has to do with the computer programs that catalog the Web sites and conduct the searches of Altavista and Google.

▶ Improve the Math and Ignore the Numbers

Using the term "blue whales" narrows things down, but Alisha also wants to protect this endangered species. Using "blue whales" will return many pages that do not talk about endangered whales.

It would be great if she could tell a search engine to find pages that talk about blue whales as an endangered species. Well, she can! Look at how Web did that search and what the results were.

Search Term	Altavista	Google	Yahoo
"blue whales" +endangered	17,400	8,100	1

The most important thing to understand is that if you use good search terms, you can ignore the fact that you get too many hits. In the example here, Yahoo might not have enough information. Google and Altavista seem to have too much, but if you do the search and look at the hits, you will see that Alisha will not have to go any further than the first page of hits to find all the information she needs.

▶ Bookmark and Move On

Another useful tool is bookmarking. When you come to a site that you think will be helpful, bookmark it. Don't spend a lot of time searching through the site now. Once you have a number of sites bookmarked, you can go back to each one and locate the information you might use.

Once you locate your sources and zoom in on the information, you can highlight important statements and copy and paste them to a word-processing document. Now you have completed step 3!

Chapter 4

Step 4:
Use of Information

4.1 Engage (e.g., read, hear, view, touch) the information in a source

4.2 Extract relevant information from a source

Now it's time to get down to the business of learning the material. During this stage, you will need to take notes. It is also important to keep track of where you got the notes, because you have to give credit for information you get from other places using citations.

Citations tell things like the title of the article, who wrote it, where it was found, when it was found, and other things. Each time you take notes, you need to include a citation that shows where you got the information.

Here is an example of some notes and a citation that Jared made about ski vacations in Canada.

Ski Vacations in Canada

The Ski Canada Web site has a page that allows you to get price quotes for ski vacations in many resorts in Canada. We can drive to most resorts in Quebec.

SkiCanada.com, *Request a Free Proposal.* SkiCanada.com. Sept. 12, 2004 <http://www.ski-canada.com/rfp/proposal.html>.

▶ Creating Citations

You cannot just write down any information about your sources. There is a special way that you must write your citations. Book citations, Web page citations, magazine citations, and interview citations are all different.

It would be very difficult to memorize all the different ways of citing sources. You need either a chart or to know a secret that I will share with you. The secret is that a good friend of Web's, Ozzie, the OSLIS computer, can help out.

OSLIS is the Oregon Schools Library Information Service. Ozzie's home page is at <http://www.oslis.k12.or.us/>. All you have to do is give Ozzie

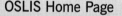

OSLIS Home Page

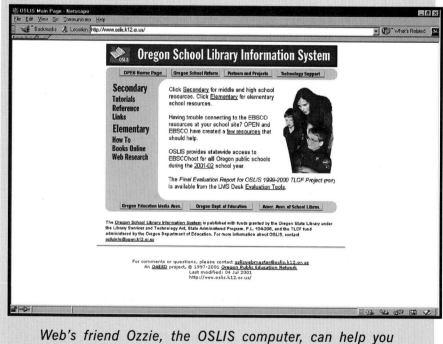

Web's friend Ozzie, the OSLIS computer, can help you create citations.

the information and he will create the citations for you automatically! Then you can just print them out or copy and paste them into your notes. It saves a LOT of time!

As far as I know, Ozzie is one of only two computers out there who will do that for you. You can try it for yourself at <http://www.oslis.k12.or.us/ elementary/howto/cited/>. Make sure you have written down the author, title, publisher, and other information about your source. Ozzie will need them to create your citation.

OSLIS Citation

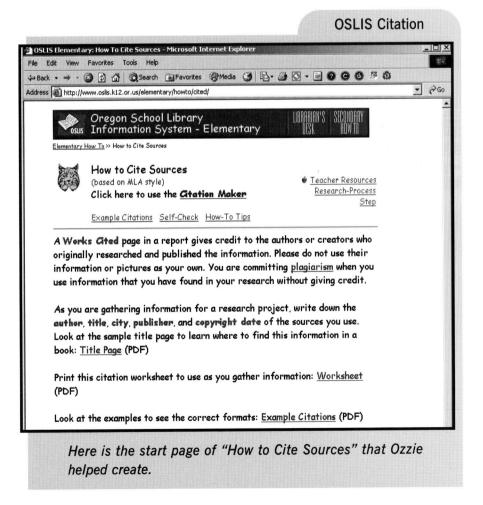

Here is the start page of "How to Cite Sources" that Ozzie helped create.

▶ Do Not Believe Everything You Read

Finding information is only the beginning of this step. Just because it is in print does not mean that it is true. Anyone can publish anything on the Internet. Researchers must know how to tell if information is true, accurate, and up-to-date. The experts agree that there are five things to look for in a Web site's information. They are accuracy, authority, objectivity, currency, and coverage.

You need to make sure that the facts are accurate and that they come from an expert. The Web site should tell you

---

Internet Addresses — Communication Facts — How Do I Do That?

Here are some sites that will help you understand the things to look for when evaluating the quality of online material.

QUICK – The Quality Information Checklist
<http://www.quick.org.uk/menu.htm>

The Internet Detective – Online Tutorial
<http://www.netskills.ac.uk/onlinecourses/tonic>

Widener University's Wolfgram Library
<http://www.widener.edu/Tools_Resources/Libraries/
Wolfgram_Memorial_Library/Evaluate_Web_Pages/659>

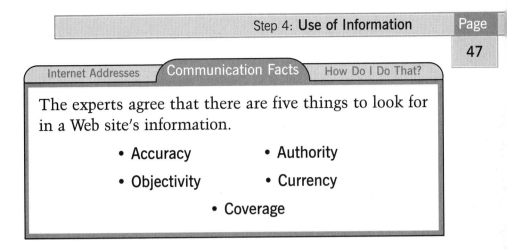

The experts agree that there are five things to look for in a Web site's information.

- Accuracy
- Authority
- Objectivity
- Currency
- Coverage

the source of the information. You should also check to see when the page was created and updated. All of these things will help you decide whether or not the site contains quality information.

Step 4 is a big one. Once you have read all the material in your sources, determined that it is of good quality, taken notes, and created citations, you are ready to begin the most challenging part. You have to organize your notes, decide what to use, and create something that will be the solution to your information problem.

Chapter 5

Step 5: **Synthesis**

5.1 Organize information from multiple sources
5.2 Present the information

Each step of the Big6 process is important, but the presentation of your work is what other people will see. While it matters how well you do steps 1–4, if you do not do a good job in step 5, you will probably have poor results. There are many ways you can show what you learned. You can write reports, build things, write songs or poems, design something, draw or paint something, or any of a dozen other possibilities.

However, the three most common ways to present your work are through a written report, a speech, or a speech combined with a multimedia presentation of some kind.

If you use computer software, you might use software such as *HyperStudio*, desktop publishing programs, *Inspiration*, or *PowerPoint*. If you do not use them correctly though, your Big6 work may not be appreciated and you may not get the credit you deserve.

▶ First Things First or First Things Second?

Look at these words...
HyperStudio presentation
Desktop publishing presentation
Inspiration presentation
PowerPoint presentation

Do you know what is wrong with the way they are written? You may think there is nothing wrong, but when they are written, the software comes *before* the presentation. Unfortunately, when people make their presentations, the same thing often happens. They spend too much time on the software and not enough time on the presentation. In other words, they put the software before the presentation when the presentation should be what you consider first.

In any presentation, you must consider your audience, your message, and your information before you worry about the software. Put your presentation before the software! Many people make the mistake of putting most of their time and effort into having fun with the sounds, slide changes, colors, and animation. They may be fun, but these things may also be distractions that take away from the points you want to make and the things you want to teach.

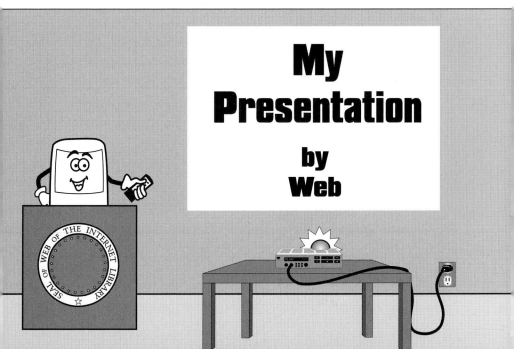

Pictures, animation, sound, and color are all very powerful tools to use in presentations, but if you use them incorrectly, they hurt your presentation rather than help it. I once heard someone say that presentation software often turns fair speakers into lousy speakers. That is because their use of sound and graphics actually takes the audience's mind away from the message of the presentation.

Instead, you should be putting the time and effort into understanding the audience and developing the message you want to send to them.

▶ Presentation Tips

I do not have enough space in this book to teach you all about how to make quality presentations with different software, but I can give you some

---

Internet Addresses | Communication Facts | How Do I Do That?

Here is a site I created that has links to all kinds of information about making presentations and using PowerPoint.

<http://www.web-and-flow.com/members/awolinsk/
    pptpoison/hotlist.htm>

If you are going to make a poster presentation, this site should interest you.

<http://www.kumc.edu/SAH/OTEd/jradel/Poster_
    Presentations/PstrStart.html>

This site helps you improve your public speaking skills.

<http://www.ku.edu/~coms/virtual_assistant/vpa/vpa9.htm>

general presentation tips and let Web point you to more information.

It does not matter what kind of software you are going to use, but there are certain things that you should keep in mind.

1. Know your material. Be sure you understand what you are trying to teach. The more comfortable you are with the material the better your presentation will be.
2. Know your audience. Create material that will interest them and help them understand your message. Do not bore them with things they already know, and make sure you explain things they do not know.
3. Plan your presentation ahead of time. Create a storyboard or outline.
4. Keep it simple and clear. Use large, easy-to-read fonts, one background, and only three or four statements per screen.
5. Use graphics, sound, or video to add value and understanding to your work. Be sure these things don't distract your audience.
6. Rehearse your presentation. Find someone to be a test audience: a parent, sibling, friend, or even your dog or cat.
7. Talk directly to your audience. Don't read your presentation.

Chapter 6

Step 6:
Evaluation

6.1 Judge the product (effectiveness)
6.2 Judge the information problem-solving process (efficiency)

Your job is not over after you make your presentation. You have to figure out how successful you were, what you did right, what you did wrong, and what you will do differently if you get a similar task in the future. The first thing you should do is to look at the way you chose to present what you learned. Did it get your message across to your audience? Could you have done better?

Once you determine how well your presentation went over, you should go back and look at each of the other five steps to see if there are things you would do differently. Here are some questions you can ask yourself about each step.

Step 1? Step 2?
Step 3? Step 4?
Step 5? Step 6?

▶ Questions You Can Ask Yourself

1. Task Definition—Did you define your task properly? Did your end result match your task definition? If not, was it the result or the task definition that was lacking?

2. Information Seeking Strategies—Were they good or did you miss some sources during brainstorming? Did you eliminate some sources that you could have used?

3. Location and Access—Did you have problems locating information? Was it because you lacked computer skills? If so, how can you improve those skills?

4. Use of Information—Did you spend enough time reading and learning your material? Did you become comfortable with your topic and information? Did you take good notes and make citations?

5. Synthesis—Did you organize your material well? Did you plan your presentation? Did you choose the best presentation method? Did you rehearse?

6. Evaluation—How successful were you? What can you do better next time?

Think about what you would do differently so next time you will be even more effective. Doing power research using the Internet and the Big6 Research Method can be a big help in solving all kinds of problems. The more you use it and evaluate how you did, the better you will get at it.

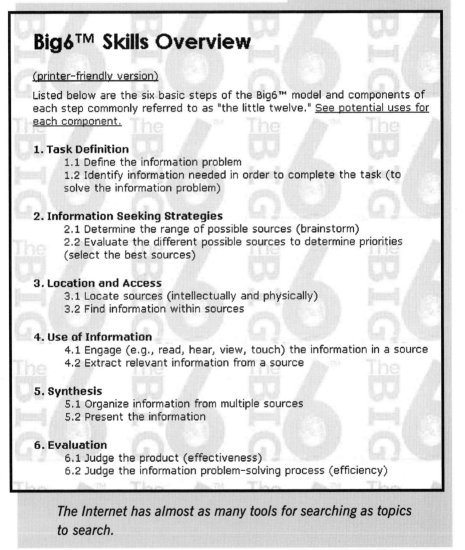

On Your Screen

Big6™ Skills Overview

(printer-friendly version)

Listed below are the six basic steps of the Big6™ model and components of each step commonly referred to as "the little twelve." See potential uses for each component.

1. Task Definition
    1.1 Define the information problem
    1.2 Identify information needed in order to complete the task (to solve the information problem)

2. Information Seeking Strategies
    2.1 Determine the range of possible sources (brainstorm)
    2.2 Evaluate the different possible sources to determine priorities (select the best sources)

3. Location and Access
    3.1 Locate sources (intellectually and physically)
    3.2 Find information within sources

4. Use of Information
    4.1 Engage (e.g., read, hear, view, touch) the information in a source
    4.2 Extract relevant information from a source

5. Synthesis
    5.1 Organize information from multiple sources
    5.2 Present the information

6. Evaluation
    6.1 Judge the product (effectiveness)
    6.2 Judge the information problem-solving process (efficiency)

The Internet has almost as many tools for searching as topics to search.

Chapter 7

Big6™
Wrap-up

The Big6 can also help you solve problems outside of school. The steps of this research method are a powerful tool. What if you were trying to plan a birthday party? How would you use the Internet and the Big6 to help? Alisha and Jared helped me find out.

I reminded them that in January it would be Grandpa's eightieth birthday and in February Grandma would also be eighty. We decided that we wanted to do something special for them and would use the Big6 to figure out what to do and how to do it.

During a half hour or so, we sat down and figured out the basic plan. Here is a summary view of what we did.

1. Task Definition

1.1 Define the information problem

We talked for a while and decided that we would give them a party. So our task was to give a party for Grandma and Grandpa.

1.2 Identify information needed in order to complete the task (to solve the information problem)

Next, we made a list of all the things we had to know before making any decisions. Should we invite just family or family and friends? How many people should we invite? How do we get the names and addresses of their friends? Do we want it to be a surprise? Should people bring presents? How much do we want to spend? What kind of food do we want? Where should we hold the party? Should we do it ourselves or have someone else do it? Who will do what? What about invitations and maps for people who would have to come a long way?

Before we even went on to step 2, we decided that a surprise party would be too hard to plan and keep secret.

2. Information Seeking Strategies

2.1 Determine the range of possible sources (brainstorm)

My brother, my sister, and I would pay for the party. So right away, we became information resources. From there we brainstormed the other sources. We could also speak with other relatives and to their neighbors and friends. Since it was not going to be a surprise, Grandma and Grandpa could also give us information.

We might be able to find information on the Internet, the phone book, the yellow pages, local newspapers, and local radio stations advertisements.

2.2 Evaluate the different possible sources to determine priorities (select the best sources)

We did not rule out any of the sources, but we thought it was unlikely we would get much help from local radio stations. We thought that we would use all of the other sources on the list. We decided to create a list of our ideas in a word-processing program to help keep track of them.

3. Location and Access

3.1 Locate sources (intellectually and physically)

We decided we would only check with Grandma and Grandpa on certain things. We would use the phone and e-mail to communicate and make most of the decisions.

The phone book and yellow pages were no problem to locate. We might even use the Internet white pages if we had a problem locating a phone number or address. (Almost any search engine has a link to Yellow Pages and White Pages.)

We found Web sites on the Internet to create maps and my sister had software to make the invitations.

3.2 Find information within sources

We would talk amongst ourselves to decide how much to spend and ask their good friends if they would help us put together a guest list. The yellow pages and the Internet could help us locate restaurants and party stores.

We decided to call and visit restaurants. We wanted to be sure that what we read and were told would match what we saw with our own eyes.

4. Use of Information

4.1 Engage (e.g., read, hear, view, touch) the information in a source

Since I lived the closest, I would call restaurants, talk to them about what we wanted, and take notes as I went. Since we had so many people coming, we wanted a restaurant that would have food for everyone, including vegetarians.

My sister would check out the Internet map sites.

We divided the other jobs up and each of us made calls and visited stores. We decided to communicate regularly using e-mail.

4.2 Extract relevant information from a source

I would narrow down the restaurant choices to three. We would make decisions on decorations,

cake, who would take pictures, and all of the other little details.

We knew that we also had to evaluate the quality of our information. Phone numbers and addresses were easy, but what about the information about the restaurants? We decided to evaluate the information we got from them by visiting each one and eating there.

5. Synthesis

5.1 Organize information from multiple sources

This is where we would divide the jobs and each of us would do our part. We had to decide on when to meet to set things up, how the room would be arranged, who would sit where, what time to start, and lots of other small details. We thought it would help to use e-mail again to send ideas back and forth and combine our ideas without having to get together in person all the time.

5.2 Present the information

Everyone would do his or her part. We would all meet an hour and a half before the guests were to arrive. We would make sure everything was ready and that we would have time to get any last minute details done. The party itself would be the presentation of the information.

6. Evaluation

6.1 Judge the product (effectiveness)

That would be easy to judge. All we have to do is watch to see if people are having fun and enjoying the food.

6.2 Judge the information problem-solving process (efficiency)

After the party was over, we would look at everything we did and ask if we would do anything differently. This was important, because we knew that there would be other family gatherings and parties coming up.

▶ The Big6™ is One Stop Shopping

In a few hours after Thanksgiving dinner, we had used the Big6 to help Jared and Alisha with their schoolwork and solve the family problem of planning a party for Grandma and Grandpa.

If there were stores for problem solving, the Big6 store would be where you would go for just about any of your problem-solving needs. You can use it for just about any problem you come across. You can use it to plan a vacation, do a research project for school, buy a birthday present for a friend, make a banana split, or set up a business. The possibilities are endless and limited only by your imagination and thought processes.

If you want some more ideas about how to use the Big6 for power research, you can visit the Resources page at the Big6 site, <http://www.big6.com/>, then click on the Resources tab. There are dozens of projects done by people who all use the Big6 method.

I am interested in hearing about your work with the Big6. Awolinsky@oii.org is my e-mail address. Feel free to e-mail me if you have comments or questions.

It has been great fun showing you about the Big6. I learned a lot. I hope what I have presented is helpful to you and that you are well on your way to solving problems of all types. After all, in not too many years, you will be in charge of your own life and might even be involved in solving some of the world's problems.

It would be great if you were able to use the Big6 and the Internet to help solve world hunger or find a cure for cancer! If you set your mind to it, anything is possible.

But until you grow up, have fun, enjoy being a kid, and may all your problems be little ones.

Glossary

bookmark—To save a site or Web page for quick reference in the future.

Boolean logic—George Boole, an English mathematician, developed this system, which is used to solve problems in logic, probability, and engineering. Boole's system shaped the development of computer logic and computer languages.

brainstorming—A way of generating many ideas in a short period of time. It requires accepting every idea that is suggested and waiting to discuss any ideas until the brainstorming session is over.

citation—A way to give credit for information from a source. It should list the title, author, where it was found, and when it was found.

concept mapping—Recording ideas as you go along in order to organize and sort them.

electronic mail (e-mail)—The most-used form of person-to-person communication on the Internet. It provides a way to communicate with people all over the world.

key words—Words used in a search for information on the Internet. The words either describe the topic or are words that one would expect to find within the Web pages to be retrieved.

meta search tools—Programs that search a number of search engines at the same time. In other words, they are search engines that actually search other search engines.

multimedia presentation—A presentation of information that uses slides, charts, graphics, animation, or other visual means.

search engine—A tool that combines large databases of information and brings back a list of sites based on key words that the user supplies.

subject trees—Also called search indexes; A tool that enables the user to make a series of choices to reach the desired information.

Further Reading

Gerry, Janet, and Allison Souter. *Researching on the Internet Using Search Engines, Bulletin Boards, and Listservs*. Berkeley Heights, N.J.: Enslow Publishers, Inc., 2003.

Harmon, Charles, ed. *Using the Internet, Online Services, and CD-ROMs for Writing Research and Term Papers*. New York: Neal-Schuman Publishers, 2000.

McGuire, Mary, et al. *The Internet Handbook for Writers, Researchers, and Journalists*. Toronto: Trifolium Books, 2000.

Roy, Jennifer Rozines. *You Can Write a Report*. Berkeley Heights, N.J.: Enslow Publishers, Inc., 2003.

Wolinsky, Art. *Locating and Evaluating Information on the Internet*. Berkeley Heights, N.J.: Enslow Publishers, Inc., 1999.

Index